W9-AUU-165

Animal Groups / Grupos de animales

A Penguin Colony / Una colonia de pingüinos

By Autumn Leigh

Traducción al español: Eduardo Alamán

Gareth Stevens
Publishing

Please visit our website, www.garethstevens.com. For a free color catalog of all our high-quality books, call toll free 1-800-542-2595 or fax 1-877-542-2596.

Library of Congress Cataloging-in-Publication Data

Leigh, Autumn, 1971-
[A penguin colony. Spanish & English]
A penguin colony = Una colonia de pingüinos / by Autumn Leigh ; traducción al español, Eduardo Alamán.
p. cm. – (Animal groups = Grupos de animales)
Includes bibliographical references and index.
Contents: Social birds = Aves sociales – Penguins of all sizes = Pingüinos de todos los tamaños – Southern living = Vida en el sur – Huge colonies = Grandes colonias – Speak up! = ¡Haciendo ruido! – Move it! = ¡En movimiento! – Penguin families = Familias de pingüinos – Caring for chicks = Cuidando a los bebés – Growing up penguin = Creciendo.
ISBN 978-1-4339-8808-0 (hardcover)
1. Penguins—Juvenile literature 2. Social behavior in animals—Juvenile literature 3. Animal societies—Juvenile literature [1. Penguins 2. Social behavior in animals 3. Spanish language materials—Bilingual] I. Alamán, Eduardo II. Title III. Title: Colonia de pingüinos 2013
598.47—dc23

First Edition

Published in 2013 by
Gareth Stevens Publishing
111 East 14th Street, Suite 349
New York, NY 10003

Designer: Sarah Liddell
Editor: Greg Roza

Photo credits: Cover, p. 1 Josh Anon/Shutterstock.com; p. 5 Ronsmith/Shutterstock.com; pp. 7 (emperor penguin), 15, 21 Jan Martin Will/Shutterstock.com; p. 7 (fairy penguin) Susan Flashman/Shutterstock.com; p. 9 Richard Burn/Shutterstock.com; p. 11 Rich Lindie/Shutterstock.com; p. 13 orxy/Shutterstock.com; p. 17 Grigory Kubatyan/Shutterstock.com; p. 19 Volodymyr Goinyk/Shutterstock.com; p. 20 Gentoo Multimedia Ltd./Shutterstock.com.

Printed in the United States of America

CPSIA compliance information: Batch #CW13GS: For further information contact Gareth Stevens, New York, New York at 1-800-542-2595.

Contents

Contenido

Social Birds

Penguins are birds that can't fly. They use their wings to swim instead—and they're very good swimmers! Penguins are some of the most social birds in the world. A group of penguins is called a colony.

Aves sociales

Los pingüinos son aves que no pueden volar. En cambio, usan sus alas para nadar. ¡Y son muy buenos nadadores! Los pingüinos son de los animales más sociables del planeta. A un grupo de pingüinos se le llama colonia.

Penguins of All Sizes

There are 17 penguin species, or kinds. Emperor penguins are the biggest kind. They can grow to be 45 inches (114 cm) tall. The smallest penguins are fairy penguins. They grow to about 17 inches (43 cm) tall.

Pingüinos de todos los tamaños

Existen 17 clases de pingüinos. Los pingüinos emperadores son los más grandes. Pueden crecer hasta 45 pulgadas (114 cm) de altura. Los pingüinos más pequeños son los pingüinos azules. Estos pueden tener hasta 17 pulgadas (43 cm) de altura.

emperor penguin/
pingüino emperador

fairy penguin/
pingüino azul

Southern Living

Wild penguins are from the Southern **Hemisphere**. Many colonies are found where it's very cold. Penguins live on islands and along the coasts of South America, Australia, New Zealand, and Antarctica. They live near water so they can find food.

Vida en el sur

Los pingüinos viven en el **hemisferio** sur. Muchas colonias viven donde hace mucho frío. Los pingüinos viven en islas y en las costas de Sudamérica, Australia, Nueva Zelanda y la Antártida. Viven cerca del agua, donde encuentran comida.

Where Penguins Live/ Dónde viven los pingüinos

Huge Colonies

Penguins often travel in small groups. However, they gather together in colonies to find **mates** and have babies. A single colony may have hundreds of thousands of penguins! One colony can cover an entire island.

Grandes colonias

Con frecuencia, los pingüinos viajan en grupos pequeños. Sin embargo, se reúnen en colonias para encontrar **pareja** y tener bebés. ¡Una colonia puede tener cientos de miles de pingüinos! Una colonia puede cubrir una isla entera.

Speak Up!

The many penguins in a colony all look the same, so they use sounds to **communicate**. This allows mates to find each other and their chicks in a crowd of penguins. They use sounds to warn each other of danger, too.

¡Haciendo ruido!

Los pingüinos de una colonia se parecen mucho entre ellos, así que usan sonidos para **comunicarse**. Esto permite que las parejas se encuentren y encuentren a sus bebés. Además usan sonidos para avisar sobre algún peligro.

Move It!

Penguins also use special movements to communicate. These movements are called displays. After making a nest, males bob their head up and down. This is a call to females. It also warns other males in the colony to stay away.

¡En movimiento!

Además, los pingüinos usan movimientos para comunicarse. Estos movimientos son despliegues. Después de hacer un nido, los machos mueven la cabeza de arriba a abajo. Así llaman a las hembras. Además evitan que se acerquen otros machos de la colonia.

Penguin Families

Female penguins lay one or two eggs once a year. In most species, the male keeps the egg warm while the female spends days or even weeks feeding at sea. When the female returns, it's the male's turn to feed.

Familias de pingüinos

Los pingüino hembra ponen uno o dos huevos cada año. En la mayoría de las especies, el macho mantiene el huevo caliente mientras la hembra pasa días, o semanas, alimentándose en el mar. Cuando la hembra regresa, es el turno del macho para comer.

Caring for Chicks

Adult penguins keep eggs warm by holding the eggs under their body and on their feet. When chicks break out of their eggs, they don't have heavy feathers like adults do. Both parents feed and keep chicks warm.

Cuidando a los bebés

Los machos mantienen el huevo caliente entre sus piernas. Cuando salen del cascarón, los bebés no tienen plumas abrigadas, como las de los adultos. Ambos padres alimentan y mantienen calientes a los bebés.

Growing Up Penguin

When the chicks in a colony get a little bigger, they often group together. This keeps them warm and safe from enemies, such as hungry seabirds. After they grow up, many penguins return to the place they were born to have their own chicks.

Creciendo

Los bebés de una colonia suelen viajar juntos al crecer. Así se mantienen calientes y seguros. Al crecer, muchos pingüinos regresan a la colonia en la que nacieron para tener sus propios bebés.

Fun Facts About Penguins/ Datos divertidos sobre los pingüinos

The earliest penguin species lived more than 58 **million** years ago.

Las primeras especies de pingüinos vivieron hace más de 58 **millones** de años.

Penguin mates often stay together for life. Some stay together for just one **breeding** season.

Las parejas de pingüinos suelen permanecer juntas de por vida. Algunos solo lo hacen por una temporada.

A penguin colony is also called a *rookery.*

Las colonias de pingüinos son llamadas *rookery* en inglés.

The largest penguin colony in the world is on Zavodovski Island in the South Atlantic Ocean. About 2 million chinstrap penguins call the island home!

La colonia de pingüinos más grande del mundo se encuentra en la isla Zavodovski en el Océano Atlántico. Cerca de dos millones de pingüinos barbijo viven allí.

Glossary

breeding: having to do with mating and giving birth

communicate: to share feelings or ideas through sounds or motions

hemisphere: one-half of Earth

mate: one of two animals that come together to produce babies

million: a thousand thousands, or 1,000,000

Glosario

comunicarse: compartir sentimientos e ideas a través de sonidos y movimiento

hemisferio (el): una mitad de la Tierra

pareja (la): dos animales que se juntan para tener bebés

millón (el): un millar de miles, o 1,000,000

For More Information/ Para más información

Books

Molnar, Michael. *Emperor Penguins.* Mankato, MN: Smart Apple Media, 2012.

Schreiber, Anne. *Penguins!* Washington, DC: National Geographic, 2009.

Websites

Emperor Penguins

kids.nationalgeographic.com/kids/animals/creaturefeature/emperor-penguin/

Learn more about emperor penguins, see pictures, and watch a video of them.

PenguinWorld

www.penguinworld.com

Read much more about the penguins of the world.

Publisher's note to educators and parents: Our editors have carefully reviewed these websites to ensure that they are suitable for students. Many websites change frequently, however, and we cannot guarantee that a site's future contents will continue to meet our high standards of quality and educational value. Be advised that students should be closely supervised whenever they access the Internet.

Nota de la editorial a los padres y educadores: Nuestros editores han revisado con cuidado las páginas en Internet para asegurarse de que son apropiadas para niños. Sin embargo, muchas páginas en Internet cambian con frecuencia, y no podemos garantizar que sus contenidos futuros sigan conservando nuestros elevados estándares de calidad y de interés educativo. Tengan en cuenta que los niños deben ser supervisados atentamente siempre que accedan a Internet.

Index

Índice